Lounge Acts

Doug Nufer

Lounge Acts

Doug Nufer

INSERT

PRESS

Los Angeles

LOUNGE ACTS

by Doug Nufer ©2013

Insert Blanc Press, 2013

The Lounge Acts lounge act ©Horist/Shoup/Nufer with Bill Horist on guitar, Wally Shoup on saxophone, and Doug Nufer on vocals, was recorded by Robb Kunz at Barça Lounge, Seattle, June 27, 2013

I'm very grateful to Mathew Timmons and to the editorial assistants at Insert Blanc Press: Byron Campbell and Saul Alpert-Abrams. And a special thanks to Wally Shoup, Bill Horist, and Robb Kunz, and to Barça Lounge for the lounge act of Lounge Acts.

and the wind and the rain and the stars and the dead and the damned and the spirit and the city and the floss and the flame and the passion and the vixen and the carpenter and the bedeviled and the injured and the large and the rock and the crow and the unreal and the bachelors and the pauper and the fury and the bear and the pendulum and the ecstasy and the gypsy and the sea and the wind and the rain and the stars and the dead and the damned and the spirit and the city and the floss and the flame and the passion and the vixen and the carpenter and the bedeviled and the injured and the large and the rock and the crow and the black and the unreal and the bachelors and the pauper and the fury and the bear and the pendulum and the ecstasy and the sea and the wind and the rain and the stars and the dead and the damned and the spirit and the city and the floss and the flame and the passion and the vixen and the carpenter and the bedeviled and the injured and the large and the rock and the crow and the black and the unreal and the bachelors and the pauper and the fury and the bear and the pendulum and the ecstasy and the gypsy and the sea and the wind and the rain and the stars and the dead and the damned and the spirit and the city and the floss and the flame and the passion and the vixen and the carpenter and the bedeviled and the injured and the large and the rock and the crow and the black and the unreal and the bachelors and the pauper and the fury and the bear and the pendulum and the ecstasy and the gypsy and the sea and the wind and the rain and the stars and the dead and the damned and the spirit and the city and the floss and the flame and the passion and the vixen and the carpenter and the bedeviled and the injured and the large and the rock and the crow and the black and the unreal and the bachelors and the pauper and the fury and the bear and the pendulum and the ecstasy and the gypsy and the sea and the wind and the rain and the stars and the dead and the damned and the spirit and the city and the floss and the flame and the passion and the vixen and the carpenter and the bedeviled and the injured and the large and the rock and the crow and the black and the unreal and the bachelors and the pauper and the fury and the bear and the pendulum and the ecstasy and the gypsy and the sea and the wind and the rain and the stars and the dead and the damned and the spirit and the city and the floss and the flame and the passion and the vixen and the carpenter and the bedeviled and the injured and the large and the rock and the crow and the black and the unreal and the bachelors and the pauper and the fury and the bear and the pendulum and the ecstasy and the gypsy and the sea and the wind and the rain and the stars and the dead and the damned and the spirit and the city and the floss and the flame and the passion and the vixen and the carpenter and the bedeviled and the injured and the large and the rock and the crow and the black and the unreal and the bachelors and the pauper and the fury and the bear and the pendulum and the ecstasy and the gypsy and the sea and the wind and the rain and the stars and the dead and the damned and the spirit and the city and the floss and the flame and the passion and the vixen and the carpenter and the bedeviled and the injured and the large and the rock and the crow and the black and the unreal and the bachelors and the pauper and the fury and the bear and the pendulum and the ecstasy and the gypsy and the sea and the wind and the rain and the stars and the dead and the damned and the spirit and the city and the floss and the flame and the passion and the vixen and the carpenter and the bedeviled and the injured and the large and the rock and the crow and the black and the unreal and the bachelors and the pauper and the fury and the bear and the pendulum and the ecstasy and the gypsy and the sea and the wind and the rain and the stars and the dead and the damned and the spirit and the city and the floss and the flame and the passion and the vixen and the carpenter and the bedeviled and the injured and the large and the rock and the crow and the unreal and the bachelors and the pauper and the fury and the bear and the pendulum and the ecstasy and the gypsy and the sea and the wind and the rain and the stars and the dead and the damned and the spirit and the city and the floss and the flame and the passion and the vixen and the carpenter and the bedeviled and the injured and the large and the rock and the crow and the black and the unreal and the bachelors and the pauper and the fury and the bear and the pendulum and the ecstasy and the sea and the wind and the rain and the stars and the dead and the damned and the spirit and the city and the floss and the flame and the passion and the vixen and the carpenter and the bedeviled and the injured and the large and the rock and the crow and the black and the unreal and the bachelors and the pauper and the fury and the bear and the pendulum and the ecstasy and the gypsy and the sea and the wind and the rain and the stars and the dead and the damned and the spirit and the city and the floss and the flame and the passion and the vixen and the carpenter and the bedeviled and the injured and the large and the rock and the crow and the black and the unreal and the bachelors and the pauper and the fury and the bear and the pendulum and the ecstasy and the gypsy and the sea and the wind and the rain and the stars and the dead and the damned and the spirit and the city and the floss and the flame and the passion and the vixen and the carpenter and the bedeviled and the injured and the large and the rock and the crow and the black and the unreal and the bachelors and the pauper and the fury and the bear and the pendulum and the ecstasy and the gypsy and the sea and the wind and the rain and the stars and the dead and the damned and the spirit and the city and the floss and the flame and the passion and the vixen and the carpenter and the bedeviled and the injured and the large and the rock and the crow and the black and the unreal and the bachelors and the pauper and the fury and the bear and the pendulum and the ecstasy and the gypsy and the sea and the wind and the rain and the stars and the dead and the damned and the spirit and the city and the floss and the flame and the passion and the vixen and the carpenter and the bedeviled and the injured and the large and the rock and the crow and the black and the unreal and the bachelors and the pauper and the fury and the bear and the pendulum and the ecstasy and the gypsy and the sea and the wind and the rain and the stars and the dead and the damned and the spirit and the city and the floss and the flame and the passion and the vixen and the carpenter and the bedeviled and the injured and the large and the rock and the crow and the black and the unreal and the bachelors and the pauper and the fury and the bear and the pendulum and the ecstasy and the gypsy and the sea and the wind and the rain and the stars and the dead and the damned and the spirit and the city and the floss and the flame and the passion and the vixen and the carpenter and the bedeviled and the injured and the large and the rock

and the wind and the rain and the stars and the dead and the damned and the spirit and the city and the floss and the flame and
the passion and the vixen and the carpenter and the bedeviled and the injured and the large and the rock and the crow and the
unreal and the bachelors and the pauper and the fury and the bear and the pendulum and the ecstasy and the gypsy and the sea
and the wind and the rain and the stars and the dead and the damned and the spirit and the city and the floss and the flame and
the passion and the vixen and the carpenter and the bedeviled and the injured and the large and the rock and the crow and the
black and the unreal and the bachelors and the pauper and the fury and the bear and the pendulum and the ecstasy and the sea
and the wind and the rain and the stars and the dead and the damned and the spirit and the city and the floss and the flame and
the passion and the vixen and the carpenter and the bedeviled and the injured and the large and the rock and the crow and the
black and the unreal and the bachelors and the pauper and the fury and the bear and the pendulum and the ecstasy and the gypsy
and the sea and the wind and the rain and the stars and the dead and the damned and the spirit and the city and the floss and
the flame and the passion and the vixen and the carpenter and the bedeviled and the injured and the large and the rock and the
crow and the black and the unreal and the bachelors and the pauper and the fury and the bear and the pendulum and the ecstasy
and the gypsy and the sea and the wind and the rain and the stars and the dead and the damned and the spirit and the city and
the floss and the flame and the passion and the vixen and the carpenter and the bedeviled and the injured and the large and the
rock and the crow and the black and the unreal and the bachelors and the pauper and the fury and the bear and the pendulum
and the ecstasy and the gypsy and the sea and the wind and the rain and the stars and the dead and the damned and the spirit
and the city and the floss and the flame and the passion and the vixen and the carpenter and the bedeviled and the injured and
the large and the rock and the crow and the black and the unreal and the bachelors and the pauper and the fury and the bear and
the pendulum and the ecstasy and the gypsy and the sea and the wind and the rain and the stars and the dead and the damned
and the spirit and the city and the floss and the flame and the passion and the vixen and the carpenter and the bedeviled and
the injured and the large and the rock and the crow and the black and the unreal and the bachelors and the pauper and the fury
and the bear and the pendulum and the ecstasy and the gypsy and the sea and the wind and the rain and the stars and the dead
and the damned and the spirit and the city and the floss and the flame and the passion and the vixen and the carpenter and the
bedeviled and the injured and the large and the rock and the crow and the black and the unreal and the bachelors and the pauper
and the fury and the bear and the pendulum and the ecstasy and the gypsy and the sea and the wind and the rain and the stars and
the dead and the damned and the spirit and the city and the floss and the flame and the passion and the vixen and the carpenter
and the bedeviled and the injured and the large and the rock and the crow and the unreal and the bachelors and the pauper and
the fury and the bear and the pendulum and the ecstasy and the gypsy and the sea and the wind and the rain and the stars and
the dead and the damned and the spirit and the city and the floss and the flame and the passion and the vixen and the carpenter
and the bedeviled and the injured and the large and the rock and the crow and the black and the unreal and the bachelors and
the pauper and the fury and the bear and the pendulum and the ecstasy and the gypsy and the sea and the wind and the rain and
the stars and the dead and the damned and the spirit and the city and the floss and the flame and the passion and the vixen and the
carpenter and the bedeviled and the injured and the large and the rock and the crow and the black and the unreal and the
bachelors and the pauper and the fury and the bear and the pendulum and the ecstasy and the gypsy and the sea and the wind
and the rain and the stars and the dead and the damned and the spirit and the city and the floss and the flame and the passion
and the vixen and the carpenter and the bedeviled and the injured and the large and the rock and the crow and the black and the
unreal and the bachelors and the pauper and the fury and the bear and the pendulum and the ecstasy and the gypsy and the sea
and the wind and the rain and the stars and the dead and the damned and the spirit and the city and the floss and the flame and
the passion and the vixen and the carpenter and the bedeviled and the injured and the large and the rock and the crow and the
black and the unreal and the bachelors and the pauper and the fury and the bear and the pendulum and the ecstasy and the gypsy
and the sea and the wind and the rain and the stars and the dead and the damned and the spirit and the city and the floss and the
flame and the passion and the vixen and the carpenter and the bedeviled and the injured and the large and the rock and the crow
and the black and the unreal and the bachelors and the pauper and the fury and the bear and the pendulum and the ecstasy and
the gypsy and the sea and the wind and the rain and the stars and the dead and the damned and the spirit and the city and the
floss and the flame and the passion and the vixen and the carpenter and the bedeviled and the injured and the large and the rock

to John Fogerty
for evey time he had to play
while people sat there drunk

Rob Roy and the Nightcaps

Rob Roy and the Nightcaps
Colt Fore and the Tee Fives
Gib Lee and the Frescas
Jim Beam and the Royal Crowns
Gar Nish and the Twists
Mick Surr and the Swizzle Sticks
Pop Off and the Grenadines
Red Dye and the Maraschinos
Dick Cull and the Jewel Lips
Miss Stir and the Boss Stun
Ray Near and the Shots
Black Jack and the Daniels
Barb Back and the Pour
Butch Mills and the Rocks
Dee Tease and the Squeezings

Honey Castro and the Bee Feeders
Dina Martina and the Stemware
Harvey Danger and the Wallbangers
Philip Glass and the Binge
Grand-Dad and the Shags
Skoal and the Gang
Ivy Poison and the Coasters
Mack Jigger and the Riling Steins

Mark Curse and the Make
Al Roy and the Keyer
Ape Pee and the Eye
Key Turk and the Wild
Fire Salve and Bay Bomb
Tan Hat and the Man
Neat Teen and the Mar
Kane Rick and the Her

Moe Hee and the Tow
Ray Most and the Fizz
Jane Bee and the Buzz
Mal Beck and the Swill
Mess Gal and the Posh
Bart Thyme and the Stool
Mel Lure and the High Life
Scott Land and the Balvenie

Tall Boys and the Ball Toys
Kay Sures and the Shakers
Dick Smink and the Mixed Drink
Gig Lure and the Liquor
Ghost Lynn and the Sloe Gin
Rock Gaffe and the Carafe
Chip Purr and the Pitcher

Dick Clark and the Minors
Bill Blass and the Old Fashions
Mae West and the Cock Tales
Queen Anne and the Imperial Pints
King James and the Jamesons
James Beard and the Sauce
Bruce Lee and the Punch
Babe Ruth and the Called Shot
Jules Verne and the Depth Charge
Mark Spitz and the Dump Buckets
James Brown and the Splits
Hart Crane and the Splash
Jeanne d'Arc and the Blue Flamers
Pope John and the Church Keys
Jim Jones and the Kool-Aid

James Bond and the Recently Disgorged
Huck Finn and the Whiskey River
Jane Eyre and the Decanters
Kay Boyle and the Toddies
Queequeg and the Harpoon

Bud Blatz and the Coors
Dick See and the Hamms
Lone Star and the Piels

Hy Ball and the Vat 69
Bound Sir and the 86ed
Sev Finn and the Seven
Graham Sport and the Six Grapes
Clare Rhett and the Five Crew Class A
Bea Girl and the Four Roses
Mack Way and the Triple Sec
Chick Kerr and the Doubles
Scott Shore and the Single Malts
Doe Zahg and the Brute Zero

Ry Plonk and the Well
Rod Gut and the Dive
Jay Surr and the Knock-backs
Mick Finn and the Pickups
Jen Mill and the Last Call

and the wind
and the rain
and the stars
and the dead
and the damned
and the spirit
and the city
and the floss
and the flame
and the passion
and the vixen
and the carpenter
and the bedeviled
and the injured
and the large
and the rock

and the crow
and the black
and the unreal
and the bachelors
and the pauper
and the fury
and the bear
and the pendulum
and the ecstasy
and the gypsy
and the sea

June Nip and the Purr
John Corn and the Barley
Sid Truss and the Bitters
Harve Fest and the Crush
Tzar Mash and the Still
Ray Shun and the Grog
Al Caw and the Haul

Mike Row and the Hops
Mack Row and the Rice
Chill Lee and the Wood Chips
Paul Yak and the New French Oak
Shell Lack and the Bathtub
Sir Plus and the Top Shelf

BU and the IPA
EU and the AOC
PD and the DUI
AA and the CTU
SP and the LCB
SS and the ATF

Bart Tend and the Dividend
Jim Flip and the Bunny Dip
Par Curse and the Hundred Points
Pete Boggs and the Cadenheads
Dee Cant and the Sediment
Lute Beggars and the Bootleggers

Tip See and the One for the Road
Chick Kerr and the Two Fingers
Goldie Lox and the Three Beers
G. Plush and the Forty Ouncers
Hooch Tote and the Fifth
Pop Topps and the Six-pack

Ice T and the Hip Hops
Carl Isle and the Brandy
Knute Dunn and the Juice
Thurston Moore and the Quench
Nat King and the Cold Porter
Oz Kerr and the Hammer Stein

Yo Han and the Bock
Yo Yo Ma and the Chilla Cella Cello
Yo Ma Ma and the Step Outside
Rin Tin Tin and the Hair of the Dog

Dinty Moore and the Stewed
Houdini and the Hollow Leg
Madonna and the Fit Chaste

Dolly Hays and Princess Tina

Marty Grah and the Hangover
Hannah Ka and the Lit
Hal O'Ween and the Spirits
Jill Lyeforth and the Coolers
Chris Muss Eve and the Midnight Service
May Day and the Cheers

Marty Grah and the Cheers
Hannah Ka and the Hangover
Hal Aween and the Midnight Service
Jill Lyeforth and the Lit
Chris Muss Eve and the Coolers
May Day and the Spirits

Marty Grah and the Spirits
Hannah Ka and the Cheers
Hal Aween and the Coolers
Jill Lyeforth and the Hangover
Chris Muss Eve and the Lit
May Day and the Midnight Service

Marty Grah and the Midnight Service
Hannah Ka and the Spirits
Hal Aween and the Lit
Jill Lyeforth and the Cheers
Chris Muss Eve and the Hangover
May Day and the Coolers

Marty Grah and the Coolers
Hannah Ka and the Midnight Service
Hal Aween and the Hangover
Jill Lyeforth and the Spirits
Chris Muss Eve and the Cheers
May Day and the Lit

Marty Grah and the Lit
Hannah Ka and the Coolers
Hal Aween and the Cheers
Jill Lyeforth and the Midnight Service
Chris Muss Eve and the Spirits
May Day and the Hangover

Marty Grah Hannah Ka Lit Coolers Jill Lyeforth
Hal Aween Chris Muss Eve Spirits Hangover May Day
And the Midnight Service Cheers

Penn Rose and the Pickled Eggs

Penn Rose and the Pickled Eggs
Joe Schlitz and the Beer Nuts
Slim Jim and the Jerky
Gib Sun and the Onions
Rick Key and the Limes
Saul Tee and the Chips
Booth Ticks and the Toothpicks

Buffy Lo and the Wings
Brett Sells and the Suds
CoCo Milks and the Coladas
Lola Loca and the Coca-Colas
Jerry Slice and the Zest
Figs Pete and the Pigs Feet

Cy Dish and the Fries
Whadja Want and the Egg in Your Beer
Rummy Spills and the Bar Rag
Ray Cell and the Frat Boys
Barb Rawl and the Sailors

Booth Ticks and the Tooth picks on Slim Jim and the jerky rummy spills. And the bar rag Lola Loca and the Coca-Colas side dish, "Whadja want—an egg in your beer?"

Penn rose Gib's son and the onion's Buffy low in the wings and the jerky rummy spills beer and the jerky pickled rummy eggs on the frat boys and the frat boys raise hell.

Joe Schlitz, Saul Tee and the chips jerry slice the rummy beer nuts and the pigs feet raise hell and the frat boys bar brawl. And the sailors? Barb Rawl and the Sailors raise hell and the frat boys sigh, dish on the fries and the rickey and the limes co-co coladas Brett sells and the zest milks the sailors' nuts.

Hy Doubt and the Vitos

Hy Doubt and the Vitos
Meg Cah and Five Spot
Eel Lee and the Shun
Kit Kat and the Klub
Zig Zag and the Field
Mack Sore and the Lees
Ron Day and the View
Bev Ridge and the Place
Red Mill and the Blue Max
Hop Vine and the Pine Box
Peter Zinn and the Doubleheader
Jane Nem and the Central
Blue Moon and the Cloud Room
Bo Wem and the Rainbow
Dee Lux and the Elite
Beast Row and the Eastlake Zoo
Cow Girls and the Buckaroo
Dream Girls and the Leg Go Show
Gord House and the City Hall
Pig Time and the Night Light
Beau Geese and the Cascadia
Lynne Does and the Oddfellows
Paul Tick and the Room
Calm Ed and the Dog House
Art Barr and the Turf
Lib Burt and the Tee
Trey Mont and the Osprey
Rip Tide and the Red Rooster
Rose Budd and the Saint Johns
Ernie Steele and the Julias
Cantor Barry and the Labor Temple Lounge
Mary Bow and the Price Is Right
Mumbling Stunk and the Stumbling Monk

Barb Band and the Spit Tune

Barb Band and the Spit Tune Wynne Doe and the Blinds Stew Lump
and the Brass Rail. Trey Stand and the Four Tops Noe Show and the
Reservation Walt Kin and the Booth. Stu Quick and the Pool Table
Yanni and the Neon Yuri Nal and the Condom Machine.

Tress Waite and the Boy Bus Dee Eye and the Man Door Dirt Tend
and the Bard. Tess Host and the Dieter Maid Sir Bounce and the
Journeymen Doris Ing and the Swing.

Skip Burr and the Corks Crew Den Blur and the Bender Mort Turr
and the Mulled. Mal Lett and the Smashed Van Tum Lim and the
Sham Pain.

Sal Loon and the Diving Ducks Down Trunk and the Town Drunk.
Mom Rhee and the Rummy Tab Lowe and the Blotto.

Paul Lee Tan and the Cosmo Gar Rita and the Marr. May Kerr and
the Boy Lure Shay Kerr and the Strained Dutch Kerr and the Rage.

Rand Hum and the Jukebox Paul Coe and the Disk Kay Rae and the
O.K. Jay Dee and the Mix DJ Riz and the Dizzy Fizz Gill Espy and
the Whiz Keys. Cho Mi and the Way to the Next Whiskey Bar. Acting
Single and the Drinking Doubles

Gay Places and the Come What May
Axis and the Wheel and the Feel
And the Sullen Gray
Faces and the Too Many Through the Day
Cy Ren and the Song
Mad Ness and the Sadness and the Great Love and the Wrong
So Sure and the Awful Week in Paris and the Bite of It
Ro Manse and the Mush Who Strive
And the Lush Life and the Small Dive
Lone Lee and the Two
Bill Lee and the Stray Horn

Hong Kee and the Tonk

Sum Whole and the Wall
Buck Gut and the It
Red Eye and the Creep Dive
El Bow and the Bend
Herse Skell and the Wrath
Night Train and the Club Car
Rip Bull and the Hobo Jungle

Tina Can and the Tapas
Lop Bess Starr and the Topless Bar
Jeer Boynt and the Beer Joint
Gyp Cloynt and the Clip Joint
Clip Strub and the Strip Club
Nib Lick and the Nineteenth Hole
Mike Night and the Mares
Verne Tav and the Brood

Dear Bargain and the Beer Garden
Doc Tale and the Lounge
Rap Tomb and the Tap Room
Sine Weller and the Wine Cellar
Peg Carty and the Keg Party
Jana Muir Wright and the Amature Night
Bart Spore and the Sports Bar
Pooh Brubb and the Brew Pub
Peer Frame and the Lanes
Candy Happers and the Turf Club

Ned Wreck and the Roadhouse
Dude Drop and the In
Fay Calf and the Café

Wynn Dee and the Three Sheets

Wynn Dee and the Three Sheets
Bo Rotch and the Ho Bea Hind and the Cork
Tay Bull and the Under
Ty Won and the On
Red Paint and the Town

Chuck Cup and the Blackouts
Breck Fast and the Blown Lunch
Cask Kit Base and the Basket Case
Al Hirt and the Feeling No Pain

Dud Moore and the Arthur
Lem Munn and the Days of Wine and Roses
Mel Land and the Lost Weekend
Nick Cage and the Vegas Exit
Bill Fields and the Great McGonagall

Jack Capp and the Pull
Al Capp and the Moonshine
Andy Capp and the Pints
Jack Webb and the Shotgun
Del Webb and the Copacabana Bail
Toots Shore and the Sex on the Beach

Pint of Plain and the Only Man

Beer Is and the Food
A Kiss and a Hug and a Shake and the Drink
Clean Well and the Lighted Place
Borne Back and the Past
Call of the Wild and the Pack
Flem and the Snopes
Limp Brick and the Hot Tin Roof

Milt Tun and the Darkness Visible
Don Tay and the Dark Wood
Chell Lee and the Darkness and Distance
Wise Blood and the Darkness Until He Was the Pin Point of Light

Père Wreck et les Revenentes
Low Cuss and the Soulless

Lee Bra and the White Noise
Dick Hins and the Worst of Times
Al Grin and the Golden Arm
Sam Spade and the Maltese Falcon
Moe Bee and the Dick

Jane Bowles and the Considerable Interest of No Great Importance
John Fowles and the French Lieutenant's Woman
Heath Cliff and the Sleepers in that Quiet Earth
Anne Surd and the Perfect Happiness of the Union
James Joyce and the Living and the Dead

Rusty Nail and the Hammered

Rusty Nail and the Hammered
Bloody Mary and the Stalk
Marty Knee and the Touchbacks
Shirley Temple and the Wagon

Drew Scriver and the Screwdriver
Campaign Shock Tale and the Champagne Cocktail
Bigger Knockers and the Knickerbockers
Cisco Power and the Pisco Sour
Ty My and the Mai Tai

Alex Sand and the Dirt
Benny Dicht and the Teen
Tom Coll and the Lens
Dag Cur and the Re:
Nick Rohn and the Eeeee

Bomb Zee and the Zombi
Sling a Pour Sing and the Singapore Sling
Guide Czar and the Sidecar
Azure Sax and the Sazeracs
Kim's Pup and the Pym's Cup

Sucky Tart and the White Cadillac
Lou Kala and the Black Russian
Moe Tato and the Red Beer
Link Beatty and the Pink Lady
Bette Rutler and the Scarlett O'Hara

Agent Orange and the Green Vesper
Jack Rose and the Golden Doublet
Amber Moon and the Blue Lagoon

Ginza Mary and the Kamikaze
Bloody Aztec and the Chupacabra
Michelada and the Cuba Libre
Nikolaschka y el Presidente

Caipirinha and the Piña Colada
Roz Elefantas and the Chi-Chi
Paloma and the Culto a la Vida
Caju Amigo and the Rabo-de-galo
Piscola and the Bellini

Moloko Plus and the Quentão
Panama and the Colombia
Pegu and the Bijou

Blue Hawaii and the Old Etonian
Cape Cod and the Moscow Mule
Missouri Mule and the Lynchburg Lemonade
Sea Breeze and the Staten Island Ferry
Bay Breeze and the Bronx
Kremlin Colonel and the Kensington Court Special
Manhattan and the Long Island Iced Tea

Irish Car Bomb and the Prince of Wales
Paradise and the Inferno

Caribou Lou and the Goldeneye
Bishop Buck and the Bernasconi
Sangria and the Modernista
Coo Vay and the French Connection

Delilah and the Hanky Panky
Salty Dog and the Woo Woo
Greyhound and the Quick Fuck
Bloodhound and the Death in the Afternoon

Dirty Mother and the Corpse Reviver
Pink Squirrel and the Monkey Gland
Mickey Slim and the Ectoplasm
Tom and Jerry and the Incredible Hulk

My Fair Lady and the Three Wisemen
Caesar and the Four Horsemen
Churchill and the 20th Century
Belladonna and the Third Rail

Bull Shot and the Hi-Fi
Pall Mall and the Last Word

Leap Year and the Grasshopper
Snake Bite and the Paralyzer
Sweet Dreams and the Painkiller
Bumbo and the Joker
Dracula's Kiss and the Sundowner
Bishop Buck and the Vesper
Yellow Fairy and the Blue Blazer
Cheeky Vimto and the Spritzer
Link Up and the Cobbler
Blow Job and the Corpse Reviver
Aviation and the Stinger
Corn 'n Oil and the Boilermaker
Robert Burns and the Flaming Homer
Imperial and the Global Warmer
Burning Bush and the Cherry Hooker
Floradora and the Dorflinger
Yellow Parrot and the Red, White, and Sapphire
Blood and Sand and the Beachcomber
Jungle Juice and the Bushwacker
Pickleback and the Benjamin's Age Reverser
B-52s and the Rock Lobster
Bayou Slime and the Red Snapper
Pot of Gold and the Irish Encounter
Leprechaun and the Shamrocker
Silver Bullet and the Crouching Tiger
Plumdog Millionaire and the Money Maker
Barbary Coast and the Modern Smuggler
Kamikaze and the Pearl Harbor
Zen Milk Bath and the Mind Eraser
Garden Jubilee and the Prairie Fire
Colorado Bulldog and the Jolly Rancher
Beatnik and the Sweaty Hipster
Alabazam and the Pumpkin Fever
Sissy Kazuki and the Freddy Fudpucker
Fresh Squeeze and the Maiden's Prayer
Gin and Tonic and the Whiskey Sour
Good Times and the Happily Ever After

Happily Ever After and the It's About That Time As Night Falls

Happily Ever After and the It's About That Time As Night Falls. And the Last Word Dobel Spicy Chili and the Weep No More. Red, White, and Sapphire and the Different Shades of Green. Root to Longevity and the Rhyme and Reason Benjamin's Age Reverser. And the Very Manly Muppet Surfer on Acid and the Swamp Water Surprise Rimbaud's Left Hand.

And the Saratoga Brace Up Blood and Sand and the Emboldened Cherry Blossom. Blondie in Blue and the Smith and Wesson Gabrielle's X-rated Kiss. And the Fins of Faith Pot of Gold and the Babel On the Rocks Hail to the Chief. And the Air Force One Love Potion #9 and the Soul Trip Tipple Look Better Naked.

And the Zen Milk Bath Black Eyed Susan and the Manhattan Love Story. Georgia on My Mind and the Misty Maple Leaf From Wine to Waikiki. And the Whispers of the Frost Marriage of Figaro and the Irish Car Bomb. Death in the Afternoon

And the Tom and Jerry The Monkey Gland and the My Fair Lady Fish House Punch. And the Dark and Stormy Kensington Court Special and the Prince of Wales. Staten Island Ferry and the Long Island Iced Tea Rock. Star Root Beer and the Yaka Hula Hickey Dula.

My Fair Lady and the Hanky Panky

My Fair Lady and the Hanky Panky
Saint Valentine and the Cherry Bitch Link Up
And the Royal Arrival Whispers of the Frost
And the Koi Woo Woo
And the Salty Dog
Naked Lady and the Maiden's Prayer

It's About That Time and the Root to Longevity
Horny Bull and the Very Manly Muppet
Bushwacker and the Bull Shot Bayou Slime

And the Southern Bride
Marriage of Figaro and the Monkey Gland
Quick Fuck and the French Connection Blow Job
And the Horse's Neck Orgasm
And the Jack Rose Ectoplasm
And the Earthquake Flaming Volcano
And the Cordial Daisy and the Savoy Affair
Manhattan Love Story

And the Witch Hunt
Burning Bush and the
Blue Blazer Delilah
And the Dirty Mother
Coronation and the Miranda
Farewell and the
Hangman's Blood

Sweet Dreams and the Muddled Rebuttal
Dirty Bird and the Dutch Dutchess
Eddy and the Envy
Soho and the Chi-Chi
Bahama Mama and the Banana Hammock
Hanky Panky and the Pall Mall
Sea Breeze and the Woo Woo
Hi-Fi and the Four Score
B&B and the Mai Tai

As Night Falls and the Plumdog Millionaire

As Night Falls and the Plumdog Millionaire
Napoleon and the Adm'ral Benbow
Link up and the Love Potion #9
From Wine to Waikiki and the Bumbo
Hail to the Chief and the Saint Valentine
Rimbaud's Left Hand and the Savoy Affair
Red, White, and Sapphire and the Hi-Fi
Rock Star Root Beer and the Geronimo

Rock Lobster and the Babel On the Rocks
Brass Monkey and the Garden Jubilee
Death in the Afternoon and the Bull Shots
Green Vesper and the Different Shades of Green
Emboldened Cherry Blossom and the Shrub
Look Better Naked and the Planters Punch

Rob Burt and the Burns
Walt Dorf and the Rhube
Bram Bull and the Brogue
Chad Wick and the Sling
May Dens and the Prayer
Lem Mun and the Drop
Ray Venn and the Rose
Red Snap and the Purr
Rock Lob and the Stir
Max Sim and the Blitz
Pearl Harr and the Burr
Mick Key and the Slim
Wolf Rum and the Punch
Joe Kerr and the Koi
Jack Rose and the Shrub
Tod Dee and the Bronx
Flip Buck and the Fizz
Royce Gose and the Fix
Beat Nick and the Smash

Teacher's Pet and the Jet Pilot
Duplex and the Red Carpet
East Side Press and the Little Black Dress
Crafty Maestro and the Tuxedo
Corazoncito and the Sombrero
Sanguinello and the Tornado
Lorraine and the Old Lay
Devil's Handshake and the Adjustable Rate
Autumn Leaves and the Envelope Please
Natural Selection and the Coronation
Bold Chieftain and the British Invasion
Fuzzy Navel and the Eiderflower Creamsicle and the Buttery Nipple
Jelly Bean and the Zorbatini
Sweet City and the Yellow Fairy
Sage Lady and the Rosemary
Talking Monkey and the Dancing Belly
Mudslide and the Jersey Flashlight
Frostbite and the Angel's Delight
Emerald Isle and the Black Stripe and the French 75
Bocce Ball and the Moonwalk
Fireball and the Cordial
Island Voodoo and the Snowshoe and the Park Avenue
Brotherly Love and the Cherub's Cup and the Immaculate
Foghorn and the Candy Corn
Mounds Bar and the Zanzibar
Central Park and the Cable Car
Modern English and the Journalist
Adonis and the Ski Lift
Porto Flip and the Julep
Biltmore and the Commodore and the Matador
Lounge Lizard and the Shaken Not Stirred
Scorpion and the Rising Son and the Lucky Deduction
Brooklyn and the Nixon and the Metropolitan
Twisted Swan and the Skillet Bomb
Ziaza and the Mimosa and the Minnehaha
Fabiola and the Speranza
Baltimore Bang and the Fat Lady Sang

and the wind and the rain and the stars and the dead and the damned and the spirit and the city and the floss and the flame and the passion and the vixen and the carpenter and the bedeviled and the injured and the large and the rock and the crow and the unreal and the bachelors and the pauper and the fury and the bear and the pendulum and the ecstasy and the gypsy and the sea and the wind and the rain and the stars and the dead and the damned and the spirit and the city and the floss and the flame and the passion and the vixen and the carpenter and the bedeviled and the injured and the large and the rock and the crow and the black and the unreal and the bachelors and the pauper and the fury and the bear and the pendulum and the ecstasy and the sea and the wind and the rain and the stars and the dead and the damned and the spirit and the city and the floss and the flame and the passion and the vixen and the carpenter and the bedeviled and the injured and the large and the rock and the crow and the black and the unreal and the bachelors and the pauper and the fury and the bear and the pendulum and the ecstasy and the gypsy and the sea and the wind and the rain and the stars and the dead and the damned and the spirit and the city and the floss and the flame and the passion and the vixen and the carpenter and the bedeviled and the injured and the large and the rock and the crow and the black and the unreal and the bachelors and the pauper and the fury and the bear and the pendulum and the ecstasy and the gypsy and the sea and the wind and the rain and the stars and the dead and the damned and the spirit and the city and the floss and the flame and the passion and the vixen and the carpenter and the bedeviled and the injured and the large and the rock and the crow and the black and the unreal and the bachelors and the pauper and the fury and the bear and the pendulum and the ecstasy and the gypsy and the sea and the wind and the rain and the stars and the dead and the damned and the spirit and the city and the floss and the flame and the passion and the vixen and the carpenter and the bedeviled and the injured and the large and the rock and the crow and the black and the unreal and the bachelors and the pauper and the fury and the bear and the pendulum and the ecstasy and the gypsy and the sea and the wind and the rain and the stars and the dead and the damned and the spirit and the city and the floss and the flame and the passion and the vixen and the carpenter and the bedeviled and the injured and the large and the rock and the crow and the black and the unreal and the bachelors and the pauper and the fury and the bear and the pendulum and the ecstasy and the gypsy and the sea and the wind and the rain and the stars and the dead and the damned and the spirit and the city and the floss and the flame and the passion and the vixen and the carpenter and the bedeviled and the injured and the large and the rock and the crow and the black and the unreal and the bachelors and the pauper and the fury and the bear and the pendulum and the ecstasy and the gypsy and the sea and the wind and the rain and the stars and the dead and the damned and the spirit and the city and the floss and the flame and the passion and the vixen and the carpenter and the bedeviled and the injured and the large and the rock and the crow and the unreal and the bachelors and the pauper and the fury and the bear and the pendulum and the ecstasy and the gypsy and the sea and the wind and the rain and the stars and the dead and the damned and the spirit and the city and the floss and the flame and the passion and the vixen and the carpenter and the bedeviled and the injured and the large and the rock and the crow and the black and the unreal and the bachelors and the pauper and the fury and the bear and the pendulum and the ecstasy and the sea and the wind and the rain and the stars and the dead and the damned and the spirit and the city and the floss and the flame and the passion and the vixen and the carpenter and the bedeviled and the injured and the large and the rock and the crow and the black and the unreal and the bachelors and the pauper and the fury and the bear and the pendulum and the ecstasy and the gypsy and the sea and the wind and the rain and the stars and the dead and the damned and the spirit and the city and the floss and the flame and the passion and the vixen and the carpenter and the bedeviled and the injured and the large and the rock and the crow and the black and the unreal and the bachelors and the pauper and the fury and the bear and the pendulum and the ecstasy and the gypsy and the sea and the wind and the rain and the stars and the dead and the damned and the spirit and the city and the floss and the flame and the passion and the vixen and the carpenter and the bedeviled and the injured and the large and the rock and the crow and the black and the unreal and the bachelors and the pauper and the fury and the bear and the pendulum and the ecstasy and the gypsy and the sea and the wind and the rain and the stars and the dead and the damned and the spirit and the city and the floss and the flame and the passion and the vixen and the carpenter and the bedeviled and the injured and the large and the rock and the crow and the black and the unreal and the bachelors and the pauper and the fury and the bear and the pendulum and the ecstasy and the gypsy and the sea and the wind and the rain and the stars and the dead and the damned and the spirit and the city and the floss and the flame and the passion and the vixen and the carpenter and the bedeviled and the injured and the large and the rock and the crow and the black and the unreal and the bachelors and the pauper and the fury and the bear and the pendulum and the ecstasy and the gypsy and the sea and the wind and the rain and the stars and the dead and the damned and the spirit and the city and the floss and the flame and the passion and the vixen and the carpenter and the bedeviled and the injured and the large and the rock

and the wind and the rain and the stars and the dead and the damned and the spirit and the city and the floss and the flame and
the passion and the vixen and the carpenter and the bedeviled and the injured and the large and the rock and the crow and the
unreal and the bachelors and the pauper and the fury and the bear and the pendulum and the ecstasy and the gypsy and the sea
and the wind and the rain and the stars and the dead and the damned and the spirit and the city and the floss and the flame and
the passion and the vixen and the carpenter and the bedeviled and the injured and the large and the rock and the crow and the
black and the unreal and the bachelors and the pauper and the fury and the bear and the pendulum and the ecstasy and the sea
and the wind and the rain and the stars and the dead and the damned and the spirit and the city and the floss and the flame and
the passion and the vixen and the carpenter and the bedeviled and the injured and the large and the rock and the crow and the
black and the unreal and the bachelors and the pauper and the fury and the bear and the pendulum and the ecstasy and the gypsy
and the sea and the wind and the rain and the stars and the dead and the damned and the spirit and the city and the floss and
the flame and the passion and the vixen and the carpenter and the bedeviled and the injured and the large and the rock and the
crow and the black and the unreal and the bachelors and the pauper and the fury and the bear and the pendulum and the ecstasy
and the gypsy and the sea and the wind and the rain and the stars and the dead and the damned and the spirit and the city and the
floss and the flame and the passion and the vixen and the carpenter and the bedeviled and the injured and the large and the
rock and the crow and the black and the unreal and the bachelors and the pauper and the fury and the bear and the pendulum
and the ecstasy and the gypsy and the sea and the wind and the rain and the stars and the dead and the damned and the spirit
and the city and the floss and the flame and the passion and the vixen and the carpenter and the bedeviled and the injured and
the large and the rock and the crow and the black and the unreal and the bachelors and the pauper and the fury and the bear and
the pendulum and the ecstasy and the gypsy and the sea and the wind and the rain and the stars and the dead and the damned
and the spirit and the city and the floss and the flame and the passion and the vixen and the carpenter and the bedeviled and
the injured and the large and the rock and the crow and the black and the unreal and the bachelors and the pauper and the fury
and the bear and the pendulum and the ecstasy and the gypsy and the sea and the wind and the rain and the stars and the dead
and the damned and the spirit and the city and the floss and the flame and the passion and the vixen and the carpenter and the
bedeviled and the injured and the large and the rock and the crow and the black and the unreal and the bachelors and the pauper
and the fury and the bear and the pendulum and the ecstasy and the gypsy and the sea and the wind and the rain and the stars and
the dead and the damned and the spirit and the city and the floss and the flame and the passion and the vixen and the carpenter
and the bedeviled and the injured and the large and the rock and the crow and the unreal and the bachelors and the pauper and
the fury and the bear and the pendulum and the ecstasy and the gypsy and the sea and the wind and the rain and the stars and
the dead and the damned and the spirit and the city and the floss and the flame and the passion and the vixen and the carpenter
and the bedeviled and the injured and the large and the rock and the crow and the black and the unreal and the bachelors and
the pauper and the fury and the bear and the pendulum and the ecstasy and the gypsy and the sea and the wind and the rain and the vixen
and the stars and the dead and the damned and the spirit and the city and the floss and the flame and the passion and the vixen
and the carpenter and the bedeviled and the injured and the large and the rock and the crow and the black and the unreal and the
bachelors and the pauper and the fury and the bear and the pendulum and the ecstasy and the gypsy and the sea and the wind
and the rain and the stars and the dead and the damned and the spirit and the city and the floss and the flame and the passion
and the vixen and the carpenter and the bedeviled and the injured and the large and the rock and the crow and the black and the
unreal and the bachelors and the pauper and the bear and the fury and the pendulum and the ecstasy and the gypsy and the sea
and the wind and the rain and the stars and the dead and the damned and the spirit and the city and the floss and the flame and
the passion and the vixen and the carpenter and the bedeviled and the injured and the large and the rock and the crow and the
black and the unreal and the bachelors and the pauper and the fury and the bear and the pendulum and the ecstasy and the gypsy
and the sea and the wind and the rain and the stars and the dead and the damned and the spirit and the city and the floss and the
flame and the passion and the vixen and the carpenter and the bedeviled and the injured and the large and the rock and the crow
and the black and the unreal and the bachelors and the pauper and the fury and the bear and the pendulum and the ecstasy and
the gypsy and the sea and the wind and the rain and the stars and the dead and the damned and the spirit and the city and the
floss and the flame and the passion and the vixen and the carpenter and the bedeviled and the injured and the large and the rock